Breakthrough
for Unanswered Prayer

by
John Avanzini

HIS Publishing Company
Ft. Worth, Texas

Breakthrough for Unanswered Prayer
ISBN: 1-878605-11-9

Breakthrough for Unanswered Prayer is a new, revised edition of the
book, *Moving the Hand of God,* first published in 1990 with over
385,000 copies in print.

HIS Publishing Company
P.O. Box 917001
Ft. Worth, Texas 76117-9001

Contents

To those who feel forgotten,

"Remember me, O Lord. . . ."

Psalm 106:4

1

How the Answer Came

> . . . concerning the work of my hands
> **COMMAND YE ME.**
>
> **Isaiah 45:11**

From the beginning of this book I want to make something perfectly clear. **I believe God answers prayer.** I also want you to know that the method of prayer I am about to teach is by no means the only one.

I offer this God-given revelation as a **solution to the church-wide scandal of unanswered prayer.** It came to me as I thought about a scripture I had once marked in my Bible.

> . . . concerning the work of my hands
> command ye me.
>
> **Isaiah 45:11**

In the margin of my Bible, I had placed a note. It simply read, **"How wonderful it would be if this could happen."**

What a statement God makes! "Concerning the work of my hands command ye me." Even though I had read it many times before, it still sounded too good to be true. Why, it seemed wrong even to imagine that the mighty God of heaven would invite us to direct the work of His powerful hand.

The Original Language Agrees

Upon checking the original language, it became obvious that the King James writers had correctly translated the words of the prophet Isaiah. God is inviting His children **to direct His hand to the place they deem it to be the most needed.**

When you understand this truth, it becomes easy to see that God really does want you to rule and reign with Him.

> **... if children, then heirs; heirs of God, and joint-heirs with Christ. ...**
> **Romans 8:17**

Suddenly, it all becomes clear. If you are to be a co-ruler with Christ, you will have to direct some of the work of God's hands.

God Actually Wants Your Advice

Don't let the thought of telling God the solution to a problem upset you. Jesus invited His disciples to do this very thing. If you remember, He asked Philip for a solution before He solved the problem of feeding the five thousand.

> **When Jesus then lifted up his eyes, and saw a great company come unto him, he saith unto Philip, WHENCE SHALL WE BUY BREAD, THAT THESE MAY EAT?**
> **John 6:5**

When Philip did not have a solution, Jesus gave Andrew a chance, and he immediately suggested they use a little boy's lunch.

> ... Andrew ... saith unto him,
> **THERE IS A LAD HERE, WHICH HATH
> FIVE BARLEY LOAVES, AND TWO SMALL
> FISHES. ...**
>
> **John 6:8,9**

Signs and Wonders Follow

As I continued my study, I found that when the children of God work with Him, mighty signs and wonders follow.

> **... They went forth, and preached every
> where, the Lord working with them, and
> confirming the word WITH SIGNS
> FOLLOWING. Amen.**
>
> **Mark 16:20**

Keep in mind that God has raised us up to work with Him.

> **[God] hath raised us up together, and made
> us sit together in heavenly places in Christ Jesus.**
>
> **Ephesians 2:6**

A Breakthrough Discovery

The next step in my study was to search the Scripture for instances where people had prayed for long periods of time without getting an answer. After considerable searching, I found two of these instances. Both were women who had long-term, unanswered prayers. They were Hannah and the widow at Zarephath. Upon close examination, I found they had something else in common. They both did the same thing, and **their action instantly turned their unanswered prayers into answered prayers.**

I must admit that when I understood what they did to move God's hand, I did not like what I saw. It was totally opposite to what I was used to hearing. Thankfully, God reminded me that His method of operation is usually opposite to our way of doing things.

> **. . . my thoughts are not your thoughts, neither are your ways my ways, saith the Lord.**
> **Isaiah 55:8**

You must always keep in mind that **neglected truth** usually doesn't set well with the Church when someone first uncovers it.

Many Lives Are Changed

I am happy to say that after just a short time of further study, God revealed from Scripture the exact way to move His powerful hand. Since I learned this truth, God has allowed me to teach it to tens of thousands of people just like you. I am happy to say that **I now receive reports daily from people who say God is regularly answering their most difficult prayer requests.**

2

Hannah's Breakthrough Prayer

. . . she vowed a vow, and said . . . remember
me. . . .

1 Samuel 1:11

The first place in Scripture I found an unanswered
prayer was in the Book of 1 Samuel. A woman named
Hannah was offering this prayer. It becomes obvious upon
close observation that she had been praying this prayer for
a long time. If you will notice, her prayer is not
unscriptural. **It is simply unanswered.** All she wants is a
child. However, no child is born.

Godly Women Pray

The Word of God tells us that Hannah is a faithful
servant of the Most High God. She and her husband go to
Shiloh and worship God each time there is a feast. During
those pilgrimages, they always make the proper sacrifices
and give generously to God.

Since we know that Hannah is a faithful worshiper of
Jehovah God, it is only reasonable to believe she is also a
woman of prayer. Because of her great desire to have a
son, we know she is constantly praying to conceive. No
doubt she rises early every morning with this special
prayer request, **"Oh, God, give me a son!** Please, God, give
your handmaiden a child." Surely she continues to call out
to the Lord throughout the day.

9

Everyone in the house knows her prayer by heart. I am sure she has asked the neighbors again and again to agree that she will conceive. All the angels of heaven know her desire. To put it bluntly, everyone in heaven and earth seems to have heard her prayer — **that is, everyone except God.**

Here we see the most heart-breaking kind of prayer. **It is an unanswered prayer!**

Violent Action

Scripture tells us that sorrow over her unanswered petition finally causes her to stop eating. At this point she makes a radical change in the way she prays. Driven by desperation, she makes one last, violent attempt to move God's hand. **Thank God, she has the sense to throw tradition to the wind** and boldly take hold of that which is rightfully hers!

Child of God, don't be turned off by the thought of taking violent action in prayer, for **the violent leap of faith** almost always brings deliverance, especially when your heaven has turned to brass.

> . . . the kingdom of heaven suffereth violence, and THE VIOLENT TAKE IT BY FORCE.
> **Matthew 11:12**

A Non-Traditional Prayer

We can see the desperation in Hannah's heart in the unusual way she forms her prayer. Her approach to God totally disregards tradition. The words she speaks can be described only as spiritual violence. Let the scoffers say what they will; one thing is sure. Hannah's new way of

10

praying swiftly moves God's mighty hand to her point of need. The Bible tells us that within hours of praying, she conceives a child. Take a moment, and read her most unusual prayer.

> **And she vowed a vow, and said, O Lord of hosts, if thou wilt indeed look on the affliction of thine handmaid, and REMEMBER ME, and not forget thine handmaid, but wilt give unto thine handmaid a man child, THEN I WILL GIVE HIM unto the Lord all the days of his life. . . .**
> **1 Samuel 1:11**

Granted, her prayer is a theological nightmare. It would quickly bring a rebuke from the scholars of today if she prayed it in their presence. Modern theologians would no doubt object because **she openly accuses God of forgetting her.** She dares to bargain with Him for an answer. I am not going to waste the precious few pages of this book to debate the theological merits of her prayer. However, God's Word does tell us **He chooses to be reminded.**

> **. . . yet will I not forget thee.**
> **Behold, I HAVE GRAVEN THEE UPON THE PALMS OF MY HANDS. . . .**
> **Isaiah 49:15,16**

I hope you caught the significance of what you just read? The Bible says your name is tattooed on the palm of God's hand. He has placed it there as a reminder so that He won't forget you. Furthermore, He plainly asks us to remind Him.

> **. . . thou shalt put the two stones upon the shoulders of the ephod for stones of memorial [reminder] unto the children of Israel: and Aaron shall bear their names before the Lord**

> **upon his two shoulders FOR A MEMORIAL [REMINDER].**
>
> **Exodus 28:12**

Notice that when he went before God, the priest wore stones upon his shoulders. The names of the twelve tribes of Israel were engraved on these stones. The Bible says God used them as a reminder of Israel. Think about that. **God used memorial stones to remember Israel.**

Moses Reminded God

> **Moses besought the Lord his God, and said, . . .**
>
> **REMEMBER ABRAHAM, ISAAC, AND ISRAEL, thy servants, to whom thou swarest by thine own self, and saidst unto them, I will multiply your seed as the stars of heaven, and all this land that I have spoken of will I give unto your seed, and they shall inherit it for ever.**
>
> **AND THE LORD [REMEMBERED and] repented of the evil which he thought to do unto his people.**
>
> **Exodus 32:11,13,14**

I am sure these verses have helped you see that, regardless of man's theology, **Jehovah God wants us to remind Him of our needs.**

Hannah Confronts God

Be assured that Hannah's new-found way of praying does not contradict God's Word. She simply expresses her true feelings about all her prayers that have gone unanswered for so long. **She feels forgotten, and she says so.** She literally storms heaven for an answer. Better said, she demands an answer from her God, and she gets one.

She Bargains With God

If you carefully study the next part of her prayer, you will see that she actually **bargains with God** for an answer.

> **. . . IF THOU WILT . . . REMEMBER ME, and not forget thine handmaid, but wilt give unto thine handmaid a man child, THEN I WILL GIVE him unto the Lord all the days of his life. . . .**
> **1 Samuel 1:11**

Please make a mental note of the extreme value of her gift. It is very precious, for it will be her first-born son.

Don't let the thought of mixing your giving and praying together disturb you. **It is not unscriptural to strengthen prayer by adding something to it.**

Fasting Added to Prayer

Why, the Lord Jesus Himself instructed His disciples to add something to one of their unanswered prayers. If you remember, **He told them to add fasting** when prayer alone had failed.

> **Howbeit this kind goeth not out but by prayer AND fasting.**
> **Matthew 17:21**

A Quick Review

How swiftly God's hand moves when Hannah boldly adds giving to her prayer! Notice carefully the decisive steps that bring her the answer.

- First, she makes a vow (a strong promise)
- Second, she asks that she be no longer forgotten
- Third, she adds giving

Let's look at her prayer one more time. I want you to have no doubt about what I am saying.

> **And she vowed a vow, and said, O Lord of hosts, if thou wilt indeed look on the affliction of thine handmaid, and remember me, and not forget thine handmaid, but wilt give unto thine handmaid a man child, then I will give him unto the Lord all the days of his life. . . .**
> **1 Samuel 1:11**

God Remembers

Now hold onto your hat as you see what takes place next. **God actually gives His written approval to her reminding Him.**

> **. . . and the Lord remembered her.**
> **1 Samuel 1:19**

There you have it in black and white! God openly states that Hannah's new prayer reminded Him of her need. I want you to notice further how quickly her answer comes. As soon as she returns home, she conceives a child.

> **. . . they rose up in the morning early . . . and returned . . . to their house . . . and Elkanah knew Hannah his wife; and the Lord remembered her.**
> **1 Samuel 1:19**

While Hannah's prayer may disturb the theologians, it is evident that it pleased God. Notice that in just a few hours, years of unanswered prayer have ended. The miracle doesn't stop there. The writer tells us that Hannah also had several other children.

> **And the Lord visited Hannah, so that she conceived, and bare three sons and two**

daughters. And the child Samuel grew before the Lord.

1 Samuel 2:21

Coincidence — I Think Not

Some will say that what you have just read is nothing more than a coincidence. However, if this same kind of prayer is repeated throughout the Scripture, we will have to accept it as a valid method of prayer.

If you feel the least bit uncomfortable with the things you have just read, I encourage you to remember the following words of our Lord.

For my thoughts are not your thoughts, neither are your ways my ways, saith the Lord. For as the heavens are higher than the earth, so are my ways higher than your ways, and my thoughts than your thoughts.

Isaiah 55:8,9

Remember, God's ways and thoughts are different from yours.

Isn't it amazing that Hannah, a simple housewife, knew more about moving God's hand than most of the Bible teachers of our day? The reason is that Hannah realized what Isaiah the prophet realized. **Man can direct the work of God's hands.**

. . . concerning the work of my hands command ye me.

Isaiah 45:11

This Is Important to You

I hope you see the importance of this revelation because it shows you how to move God's hand **to the point of your greatest need.**

Please take a brief moment and focus your attention on the powerful testimony of someone else who did exactly as Hannah did and turned an unanswered prayer into an answered one.

Dear Brother John,

My son, Casey, has always been a problem. He never responded well to discipline. His grades were poor, and he never had any real friends. My heart would break for him. By age sixteen, he had dropped out of school and was smoking and drinking.

I married a Christian man. Our construction business was doing poorly. A friend gave me a copy of your book, **Powerful Principles of Increase.** I thought, "I don't have much to lose and a lot to gain." **I sent $100 and the results were astounding and almost overnight.**

A few months later I got a copy of your book, **Moving the Hand of God .*** One sentence really stirred me. It asked the question, **"Do you have a wayward child?"** I made a vow. While the answer didn't come immediately, things did start to change. It began with me. Every time my son would mess up, I'd remind the Lord of the memorial prayer I had made.

One night my son came into the kitchen and broke into tears. He handed me a $50 bill and said, "Mom, I want you to tithe this money for me. **I was about to spend it on**

---

* *Breakthrough for Unanswered Prayer* is a new, revised edition of the book, *Moving the Hand of God,* first published in 1990.

drugs to sell when something powerful stopped me. I just couldn't do it."

I hugged him and we both cried. Since then he's got a good job. He is also continuing his schooling. **He has quit smoking and drinking.** My son now thanks me regularly for sharing the Lord with him. Casey is not perfect, **but my prayer for him is memorialized in heaven, and it just keeps on working.**

A.G.
Los Alamos, CA

3

A Widow Stops the Death Angel

> ... behold, I am gathering two sticks, that I
> may go in and dress [the meal and oil] for me
> and my son, **THAT WE MAY EAT IT, AND DIE.**
> 1 Kings 17:12

Let's now focus our attention on a woman who is just hours from death. Like Hannah, she is a godly woman. Upon close examination it becomes evident that she has been praying for a long time. Her unanswered prayer **is about a food supply that is running out rapidly,** but nothing has happened. God has not moved.

This is a special woman, for God has planned a visit between her and the great prophet, Elijah. Pay close attention to what she has to do to get her prayer answered. With the help of her man of God, **she adds the missing ingredient** that quickly turns her unanswered prayer into **a starvation-breaking prayer.**

You will find this widow to be one of the most spiritual women mentioned in the Bible. Scripture tells us that she walked so closely to her God that He manifested Himself to her. The Bible says that when He spoke to her, He spoke in an audible voice. Notice that He also entrusted to her the care of His choice prophet, Elijah.

. . . behold, I have COMMANDED a widow woman there to sustain thee.
1 Kings 17:9

A Single Mother

With the Scripture clearly establishing the relationship between this dear woman and God, let's now take a closer look at her personal circumstances. We are told **she is a widow,** and to complicate that situation, she is also **a single mother.** She has a son.

Of all the hardships single mothers face, I am convinced the most pressing is that of keeping food on the table. This responsibility lets us know she is a praying woman. There can be no doubt about it. **The dwindling barrel of meal** mixed with the hunger of her son causes her to pray night and day. However, in spite of her relentless prayer, **the evil day still comes.** It is the day she hears the awful sound of the cup scraping **the bottom of her barrel.**

Can't you just hear her as she prays, "Oh, Lord, my son and I need a miracle. If you don't help us, we will surely perish. Oh, God, can't you see we are running out of food? **Lord, have you forgotten us?"**

Please take note: hers is a scriptural prayer. Jesus Himself teaches us to pray for our daily bread.

Give us this day our daily bread.
Matthew 6:11

The Misery of Unanswered Prayer

Try as she may, absolutely nothing happens as she prays. Every day things just keep going from bad to worse.

Then the dreaded day arrives when she has to face the fact that God is not answering. The barrel is just one meal away from being empty. She can hear the wings of the death angel at her door. The eleventh hour has come, and God's hand has not moved. Unless there is an immediate change, she and her son will die.

The icy hand of fear now firmly grips her heart. It is that most devastating kind of fear, **for it is the fear of insufficiency.** Her hopelessness is only intensified by the feeling that God has forgotten her.

All of a sudden her attention is drawn to a familiar figure in the distance. It's her man of God, and she knows he is coming to her house to receive an offering. If only he had come when the barrel was full, she would have enjoyed his visit so much. With only scant rations remaining in her little cup, she hears a voice from the spirit world. The devil tells her, **"All the preacher wants is to take from you."** Upon hearing these words, she makes a crucial decision. **She will not feed the prophet.** She will not share her last meal with the man of God.

A Cup of Water

Elijah begins his conversation with a simple request.

> . . . Fetch me, I pray thee, A LITTLE WATER in a vessel, that I may drink.
> 1 Kings 17:10

Without hesitation she moves to fetch it. However, even as she goes, she dreads hearing his next words. She knows exactly why he has come. The words of instruction from God are still ringing in her ears. He has already told her to feed the prophet.

> . . . I [God] have commanded a widow
> woman there to sustain thee.
> 1 Kings 17:9

She knows that any moment now, Elijah will break the silence and ask for food.

Then he speaks the dreaded words. **"Bring me a morsel of bread."** Had Elijah asked for anything else, she would have gladly given it to him. He could have asked for a change of clothing. He could have asked for a place to rest from his journey — anything except something to eat. You see, unanswered prayer has left her with an empty barrel, and **it's hard to give the last you have.**

Her Faith Breaks

Like a huge tidal wave, the disappointment of multiplied hours of unanswered prayer comes crashing against her soul. When she finally answers Elijah, she is face to face with the ugliest part of unanswered prayer, **for it is faith-breaking prayer.** Hear her as she speaks.

> . . . As the Lord THY GOD liveth, I have not
> a cake, but an handful of meal in a barrel, and a
> little oil in a cruse. . . .
> 1 Kings 17:12

Carefully notice that she doesn't say, "as the Lord **my** God liveth." Instead she says, "as the Lord **thy God** liveth." These words tell us that her once strong faith has been broken. Unanswered prayer has done its ugly work. She no longer refers to the great Jehovah as her God. **He is now nothing more to her than the prophet's God.**

You are possibly already experiencing some of these same feelings. The bottom of your barrel may be appearing. **The cold feeling of being forgotten** is becoming harder and harder to cast down. Be careful, for that feeling **has the power to break your faith.**

Fear Not

Pay close attention to how Elijah helps this woman. First, he disconnects her from the devil's pipeline as he instructs her not to fear (1 Kings 17:13).

Oh, child of God, you must learn that fear is a conduit that links your life to the kingdom of darkness! It literally turns you into a **negative magnet,** drawing all the torments from the devil directly into your path. The Word of God says that whatever you fear becomes almost impossible to avoid.

> . . . the thing which I greatly feared is come
> upon me, and that which I was afraid of is come
> unto me.
>
> **Job 3:25**

When he faced tragedy in his life, Job identified the root cause of all of his problems as fear. It magnetically drew misery into his life. It ushered in poverty where there had been abundance, sickness where there had been health, and death where there had been life.

Fear Is Not From God

Don't be fooled. Fear never comes from God!

> For God hath not given us the spirit of
> fear. . . .
>
> **2 Timothy 1:7**

The worst thing you can possibly do in the time of insufficiency is to allow fear to enter into your being. It will draw even more insufficiency into your life. When fear rises up, you must cast it off immediately, for it never brings any good thing with it.

Watch Your Mouth

Elijah's second words of instruction to the woman are equally important.

> . . . go and do as thou hast said. . . .
> **1 Kings 17:13**

If you notice, the woman had spoken only one positive word to Elijah. She had said she and her son were going to eat.

How important the prophet's words are! If she ignores them and continues speaking of death and insufficiency, God will not work the miracle she needs. Never forget our Lord's teaching about the things you say.

> . . . whosoever shall say unto this mountain, Be thou removed, and be thou cast into the sea; and shall not doubt in his heart, but shall believe that those things which he saith shall come to pass; HE SHALL HAVE WHATSOEVER HE SAITH.
> **Mark 11:23**

When insufficiency tries to come upon you, do not speak of its power. Speak only of God's promised supply.

Giving Is Added

At this point the widow lacks only one thing. **It is the ingredient that will immediately move God's hand into her empty barrel.** It goes without saying that she has prayed a mountain of prayers. However, it isn't until her man of God causes her to add giving to her prayer that God moves. Yes, that's right. Just like Hannah, **it is her giving that activates God.**

> **. . . make me thereof a little cake first. . . .**
> **1 Kings 17:13**

Child of God, please allow this truth into your spirit. When the man of God appears in your life, **even if he comes with an offering plate in his hand,** he has not come to spoil your picnic. Don't let the devil tell you he has come to add to your misery. Giving has always been an essential part of receiving from God. Notice that Jesus tells us the same thing.

> **GIVE, AND IT SHALL BE GIVEN UNTO YOU. . . . For with the same measure that ye mete [give] withal [to others] it shall be measured to you again.**
> **Luke 6:38**

Elijah's words to the woman are straightforward. The hand of God will move to her empty barrel if she will only add giving to her prayer.

> **. . . MAKE ME THEREOF A LITTLE CAKE FIRST. . . .**
> **For thus saith the Lord God of Israel, The barrel of meal shall not waste, neither shall the cruse of oil fail, until the day that the Lord sendeth rain upon the earth.**
> **1 Kings 17:13,14**

Refreshing Comes

With these powerful words spoken, the woman's spirit begins to revive. Her negative, self-centered outlook quickly turns into a faith-filled spirit of giving. Her change of attitude speeds the hand of God into the midst of her dwindling supply.

> **And she went and did according to the saying of Elijah: and she, and he, and her house, did eat many days.**
> **And the barrel of meal wasted not, neither did the cruse of oil fail. . . .**
> **1 Kings 17:15,16**

There is no way to deny it. When she adds giving, **she immediately energizes** her previously unproductive prayer.

Please don't miss this important fact. The gift she gives is extremely valuable. She gives the last bit of food she has!

Supply Comes

Just try to imagine how happy it makes her to see her barrel begin to strain from the abundant supply God is pouring into it! Imagine how thankful she is that she has a man of God **who has the integrity** to tell her what God's Word says about giving and receiving. If you think about it, you will have to conclude that **her giving cancels the death angel's visit.**

> **And the barrel of meal wasted not, neither did the cruse of oil fail, according to the word of the Lord, which he spake by Elijah.**
> **1 Kings 17:16**

Here we have another example of desperate prayer that goes unanswered, until the woman mixes it with generous giving. As soon as she does, the hand of God moves swiftly to meet the family's need. It worked for Hannah, and now you see it working for the widow at

Zarephath. Surely these two cases are confirmation of the truth God is trying to reveal to your spirit. However, rest assured that there are many other examples. God's Word literally abounds with illustrations.

Before going on to the next chapter, allow the following testimony to add its voice to the growing list of those who have quickly moved the hand of God by mixing their giving and praying together.

Dear Brother John and Sister Pat,

Thank you, for my burdens are lifted. **God has answered my memorial prayer for my daughter and her husband.** They are experiencing a newness in their marriage which they cannot explain, but I can. It's my memorial prayer at work.

When your office called, I was not feeling too good. One of the people in your Partner Love Center* prayed with me, and I felt a surge of God's energy flood my body. **I have not been the same since that phone call.**

I am now making my second memorial prayer. It will be for my flower business. Please be in agreement with me that my orders will increase. I want this increase so that I can be a blessing to you and others in this end time.

Everybody who knows me can tell there's a difference in my health and energy level **since we started in memorial prayer** with you. They are amazed that **a seventy-five-year-old lady** can do as much as I now do. **What they need is to understand memorial prayer as I do.**

M.M.
Pocomoke City, MD

---

*   If you would like someone to pray with you, call the Partner Love Center at (817) 222-0011.

4

An Emergency Prayer

... If thou shalt ... deliver ....
... whatsoever cometh forth of the doors of
my house ... I will offer it. ...
Judges 11:30,31

How would you pray if God chose you to lead His army into a real shooting war, and just as the battle began, **one of your strategic battalions refused to fight** and went home? This situation actually happened to a man named Jephthah.

Building an Army

Following standard procedures, Jephthah prepares the nation of Israel for war. He marches through the land gathering recruits as he travels toward the battlefront. As soon as he forms his army, he proceeds directly to the camp of the Ammonites and challenges them to fight.

Please keep in mind that Jephthah is the divinely recognized judge of Israel and is doing all this at God's command.

> Then the Spirit of the Lord came upon Jephthah, and he passed over Gilead, and Manasseh, and passed over Mizpeh of Gilead, and from Mizpeh ... he passed over unto the children of Ammon.
> Judges 11:29

Betrayed by Brothers

While the scriptural account gives few details, **it is clear that something goes wrong.** The exact cause of Jephthah's problem would go undetected except for two verses in chapter twelve. There we learn that the tribe of Ephraim disobeys Jephthah's command and leaves him at the mercy of the enemy.

> **. . . WHEN I CALLED you [Ephraim], YE DELIVERED ME NOT out of their hands.**
> **Judges 12:2**

When the tribe of Ephraim rebels, the balance of power swings into Ammon's favor. Suddenly Jephthah is faced with grim reality; unless he can get God to intervene immediately, the Ammonites will destroy the army of Israel.

When Time Is of the Essence

When the enemy is about to overthrow you, **the speed at which God moves becomes very important.** With only moments to spare, Jephthah must move God's hand, and he must move it quickly. If he fails, or if God hesitates, all will be lost. Notice carefully how he words this most important prayer.

> **And Jephthah vowed a vow unto the Lord. . . .**
> **Judges 11:30**

Please keep in mind that **this is the prayer of a desperate man.** He is on a real battlefield with the death angel just a heartbeat away.

The Most Effective Prayer

Notice that Jephthah has a choice of using any form of prayer. However, he chooses to approach God **by mixing his prayer with the best gift he can possibly give.**

> **And Jephthah VOWED A VOW unto the Lord, and said, IF THOU SHALT WITHOUT FAIL DELIVER the children of Ammon into mine hands,**
> **Then it shall be, that WHATSOEVER COMETH FORTH OF THE DOORS OF MY HOUSE TO MEET ME, WHEN I RETURN in peace from the children of Ammon, SHALL SURELY BE THE LORD'S, and I will offer it. . . .**
> **Judges 11:30,31**

The Eleventh Hour Is Not for Experimenting

Take special notice that this is not the time for Jephthah to try out some new method of praying. There are only a few precious moments to call out to God. Without hesitation, his prayer must move God's hand. If it goes unanswered, all of Israel will perish. **There will be no second chance to pray.** Even as the Ammonites are breaking through Israel's first lines of defense, Jephthah speaks the type of prayer he trusts the most. He chooses a special prayer, **one that is energized with an offering.**

A Most Liberal Offering

Notice the value of the offering Jephthah makes. It is the most liberal offering possible. With deliberate words, he opens the entire inventory of his possessions to God. Without reservation, he gives God the authority to take whatever He will from among his belongings.

> . . . whatsoever cometh forth of the doors of
> my house . . . I will offer it. . . .
> **Judges 11:31**

Now, let's see if God honors Jephthah's prayer.

> So Jephthah passed over unto the children
> of Ammon to fight against them; AND THE
> LORD DELIVERED THEM INTO HIS HANDS.
> **Judges 11:32**

His Only Daughter

In case you do not know, let me tell you the first thing
to come forth from his house. **It is his only child,** a
precious daughter. If Jephthah keeps his promise, she will
have to serve in God's house for the rest of her life. She
will never have children. There will be no lineage of
Jephthah left in the earth. How great this man's offering
will be!

Does Jephthah fulfill his vow? The Word of God says
he does.

> And . . . her father . . . did with her
> according to his vow which he had vowed. . . .
> **Judges 11:39**

A Three-fold Cord

With the account of Jephthah's gift-laden prayer, I
have now placed before you three powerful Bible
examples of people who, by mixing their giving and
praying together, **quickly moved the hand of God to the
point of their greatest need.** We first saw this form of
prayer in the life of Hannah. Then the widow at Zarephath
used it. Now we have seen Jephthah use it. In each of these
desperate situations, God's deliverance came quickly.

As you let the clear truth of God's Word **override the tradition of men,** you will conclude that this ancient biblical method of praying is among the most powerful that God's Word presents.

Let's take a moment to enjoy the following testimony.

Dear Brother John,

After reading *Moving the Hand of God,* * I knew I needed to make a memorial prayer, but I didn't have the money. In 2 Corinthians 9:10, the Word says He will always supply seed to the sower. So I said, "Lord, I need some money to give with my prayer." **Miraculously He supplied the seed for me to sow.**

The memorial I made was for my daughter and her marriage. Her husband would not go to church, and he was abusive to her. My daughter and I had prayed. My friends had also prayed, but nothing happened. Then I made my memorial prayer, **and the hand of God moved.**

My son-in-law recently told me he had changed in two ways. He said, "I now have a new heart for my wife and for the things of God." When we mixed our praying and giving together, God's hand moved. **Long-term prayer quickly became answered prayer.**

J.H.
Washington, D.C.

---

*   *Breakthrough for Unanswered Prayer* is a new, revised edition of the book, *Moving the Hand of God,* first published in 1990.

5

A Roman Soldier Builds a Memorial

> ... Thy prayers and thine alms are come up
> for a memorial before God.
>
> **Acts 10:4**

Please read this chapter carefully. It contains the clearest information in Scripture about the mixing together of praying and giving. In it the angel of the Lord tells us that God calls this type of prayer **"memorial prayer."**

A Gentile Seeks God

It is now time to introduce **the most important scriptures in this teaching.** They are about a man named Cornelius. While the information about him is limited, it is explicit. He is a most significant figure in the New Testament, for he is the first Gentile Christian.

The account tells us that Simon Peter first hears of God's plan to save the Gentiles while on a rooftop in the city of Joppa. In a powerful vision, God shows him that he must be willing to present the gospel to all the inhabitants of the world. At this same time, an angel visits Cornelius and tells him to invite the Apostle Peter to his home.

A Faithful Gentile

Cornelius is a devout man, one who sincerely desires to have a personal relationship with God. He believes Jehovah is the one and only living God. He faithfully puts into practice all he can learn about Him. The Scripture is careful to mention his generosity in the giving of his finances. It goes on to tell us that he prays to receive more knowledge about the Lord.

While Cornelius prays, an angel appears to him and **gives him the clearest explanation found in Scripture about prayer that is mixed with giving.**

Hear the words the angel speaks.

> **... Thy prayers and thine alms [giving] are come up for a memorial before God.**
> **Acts 10:4**

The angel tells Cornelius that when God saw his prayer mixed together with his giving, it became a memorial in His sight.

Don't misunderstand. Prayer is great and powerful by itself. Giving is also very powerful. However, God's Word says **when these two powerful acts are mingled together, they become even greater.** They become memorial prayer.

A Perpetual Reminder

The angel doesn't stop with this statement. He tells Cornelius even more about this powerful type of prayer.

> **... Cornelius, thy prayer is heard, and thine alms are had in remembrance in the sight of God.**
> **Acts 10:31**

Take note of the special wording the angel uses, "are had in remembrance." The angel tells us that memorial prayer literally **takes up permanent residence in the sight of God.** The Amplified Bible emphasizes this truth even more by saying that this kind of prayer is **"preserved before God** [so that He heeds **and is about to help you]"** (Acts 10:31).

Please take time to digest this thought, for when you understand it fully, **your prayer life will never be the same again.**

Let's now look at the verse that follows:

> **Send therefore to Joppa, and call hither Simon, whose surname is Peter.** . . .
> **Acts 10:32**

Don't miss the significance of what the angel is saying to Cornelius. He says, "Send therefore." He tells Cornelius that because he mingled his prayer with his generous giving, he can now send for the Apostle Peter. Let me paraphrase what the angel said: Your prayer mingled with your giving has placed your request in perpetual remembrance before God. Because you prayed and gave, you may now send for the apostle.

Clarity Comes

Notice how these few words spoken by the angel clarify the things we have been learning. They teach us that prayer mixed with giving **not only amplifies the power of the prayer, it also prolongs its effectiveness.** You know this type of prayer has much influence with God, for we see it move God's hand to the rooftop in Joppa, and bring Simon, a Jew, to the home of Cornelius, a Gentile.

Now that you have a better understanding of memorial prayer, you can put it to work in your own life with more confidence. In the same way that Cornelius **supercharged his prayer,** you can now begin **to supercharge yours.**

Try thinking of memorial prayer in this way. It is as if you are raising a large stone of remembrance before God, and permanently etched into it are the words of your prayer! Your Bible tells you this type of prayer brings a speedy answer.

> . . . He [God] heeds and is about to help you.
>
> **Acts 10:31, Amplified**

A Parallel From My Youth

When I was a young man, I worked as a brick layer. In that trade, men use a cement-like substance called "mortar." They place it between bricks to hold them together.

Mortar has a special composition. It begins as powdered cement which must be thoroughly mixed with water. If the powder alone is put between the bricks without the water added, **the wind will quickly blow it away.** On the other hand, if only the water is put between the bricks, **it will soon evaporate.** However, when the powder is properly mixed together with the water, in a short time it becomes hard as concrete. In this form **it becomes perpetual** and stays between the bricks as long as the wall stands.

I have laid the brick into walls that are now **over thirty years old,** and the mortar is still in place. In the nation of

Israel, I have seen mortar that was placed between stones **before Jesus walked the earth.**

Strange as it may seem, brick walls don't stand the test of time because of the bricks. **They stand because of the mortar** which is made by mixing cement and water together. By itself cement is a powder, and water is a liquid. However, when they are mixed together, **they become solid and perpetual.** They bear perpetual testimony of the desire of the one who made the wall.

The Mortar of Your Memorial

When they are mixed together, your prayer and your offering produce something bigger than either can produce by itself. They form a memorial prayer, a supercharged prayer that rises up and **perpetually presents** the desire of your heart before God.

Hannah Did It

Hannah's vow to God, added to her prayer, caused her request to become a memorial. It immediately gave her prayer for a son a place of prominence in God's sight. Then the Scripture clearly states that the Lord remembered her and sent His hand to open her womb. Hannah built a memorial prayer!

The Widow Did It

It was well past the eleventh hour for the dear widow at Zarephath when she gave her offering to the man of God. With her act of giving, she immediately turned her previously unanswered prayer into a memorial prayer. Just as quickly as she did it, the hand of God moved to fill her empty cupboard. The widow at Zarephath built a memorial prayer!

Jephthah Did It

As he faced sudden death, Jephthah vowed to give anything he had if God would only deliver him. Without hesitation he committed his life and the lives of his men to the power of memorial prayer, and just as quickly, the Lord delivered the enemy into his hands. Jephthah built a memorial prayer!

Valuable Offerings

Please do not fail to notice the extreme value of each of these offerings. One woman gave her firstborn son. Another gave the last bite of food she had. A national leader gave God whatever He wanted of his possessions. This same thing holds true with Cornelius. A continual stream of generous offerings drives his prayer ever upward until God answers by sending a divinely commissioned apostle to his door.

With the introduction of Cornelius, we find **the clearest explanation of this previously neglected type of prayer.** We must now add his name to our list, for he built a memorial prayer that brought him the distinct honor of being the first Gentile Christian.

There's More to Come

Please don't think you now know all there is to know about this subject, for our study is far from complete. However, before going on, take a moment and enjoy another victory testimony that came through the use of memorial prayer.

Dear Brother John,

My husband and I have struggled for the entire fourteen years we have been married. In April we decided to go to Tulsa for a Rhema Get-Acquainted Weekend. We found what God wanted for us. We returned home and began packing, having garage sales, applying for jobs in Tulsa, and closing down our business. When we sent you the memorial prayer money in August, **we had absolutely no money for the move.**

From the sale of a car and an unexpected insurance check, James went for an interview, but they gave him a "We'll get back to you" response. We found a buyer for our business, and the sale provided enough money for the move. We hunted for a place to stay, but we were always too late or too broke. Then God reminded us of a number we had seen. We called the real estate agent and we found the perfect house.

James called that night and found **he had got the job,** making him the first full-time employee the firm had hired in ten years. They are paying him $10 per hour, **which is $3 higher than usual.** The next day we went to get our mail at the post office and received **an unexpected check for $500,** and the next week **there was another one for $600.** We also had **a $200 debt cancelled** during this time. **Our memorial prayer worked quickly and effectively.**

P.C.
Tulsa, OK

6

Two Mites Draw God's Attention

> ... she of her want did cast in all that she
> had. ...
> #### Mark 12:44

Most Christians are surprised to learn where Jesus is when He meets the widow with the two mites. The Word of God says He has seated Himself in front of the treasury and is watching the people give. **Yes, you have read correctly.** Jesus is in front of the offering plate, observing the people as they give their money.

> ... Then he sat down IN FRONT OF THE
> COLLECTION BOX.
> #### Mark 12:41, Williams

Notice that He is observing not only how much they give. He is especially interested in their innermost feelings as they give.

> ... Jesus sat over against the treasury, and
> beheld how the people cast money into the
> treasury: and many that were rich cast in much.
> And there came a certain poor widow, and
> she threw in two mites, which make a farthing.
> #### Mark 12:41,42

All Offerings Are Not Equal

Jesus acknowledges a vast difference between the offerings of the rich and the offering of this poor widow.

The rich are giving significantly larger amounts of money than she is. In spite of this difference, **our Lord determines that her offering is larger than any of theirs.**

The reason for this conclusion is that the money the rich are giving is of a different level of importance to them from the money she is giving. Scripture tells us the rich donors are giving their large offerings **out of their abundance (their excess funds).** They are actually giving out of money they have left after they have met their basic needs. Their offerings are coming from the **discretionary part** of their income.

> For all they did cast in of THEIR ABUNDANCE....
> **Mark 12:44**

However, the widow's offering is made up of a different kind of money. **She is giving out of her bill-paying money.** The Bible says her offering is made up of the money she is living on.

> ... she ... did cast in all that she had, EVEN ALL HER LIVING.
> **Mark 12:44**

Giving to Receive

Being an Israelite, the widow knows that Jehovah is a good God and wants to bless her. She also knows from His Word that if she gives generously to Him, He will be more than generous to her.

How valuable this woman's offering is, for she must depend upon God to replace the money she is giving so that she can meet the needs she has that very day.

Casting Down Evil Imaginations

Try to imagine the thoughts that go through her mind as she approaches the offering plate. How frustrating it must be to see the rich tossing in their large sums of money. Why, any one of their offerings would easily satisfy her every desire. Can't you just hear the devil as he tries to tell her how insignificant her offering is? "Why, compared to their large donations, **God won't even notice your pitiful, little offering."**

Thank God that just as quickly as these thoughts come, she is able to cast them down. Then, in a sudden burst of faith, **she throws in her money!**

> **. . . she THREW IN two mites. . . .**
> **Mark 12:42**

Notice how quickly her action ends the argument with the devil. His mouth is shut for good on the matter, for her violent action has totally committed her to God for an answer. **She has given, and she's given big!**

Violent Action Brings Attention

The Bible tells us the abrupt action of the widow immediately catches the attention of our Lord.

> **And he called unto him his disciples, and saith unto them, Verily I say unto you, That this poor widow hath cast more in, than all they which have cast into the treasury.**
> **Mark 12:43**

Jesus has seen what she has done, and **He now fixes His attention on her.**

She Wants Something

If you look closely, you will see that the Lord not only acknowledges the extreme value of her gift, but also realizes she desperately wants something from Him. Yes, she has attached a prayer to her giving. Watch closely or you will miss it.

> . . . she of her WANT did cast in all that she had. . . .
>
> Mark 12:44

Those few words from Jesus let us know that the widow's money is part of something bigger than just an offering. It is a memorial prayer, **for she has mingled it with a special desire she has in her heart.** She wants something from her God.

We don't know how much theology this woman knows. However, one thing we do know. **She thoroughly understands** God's plan of mixing giving and praying together. The very fact that she gives everything she has tells us she believes memorial prayer works. Scripture proves her to be right, for as soon as she gives her offering, Jesus acknowledges that she wants something from Him.

> . . . she of her want did cast in all. . . .
>
> Mark 12:44

God Made a Memorial

Please let these next few words minister to you. **God understands** how it feels to want something. You see, **He wanted you.** In fact, to get you, God did exactly what this poor widow did. **He mixed His giving with His desire.** Because of His great desire for you, He gave His only Son on the cross of Calvary.

> For God so loved the world, that he gave his
> only begotten Son, that whosoever believeth in
> him should not perish, but have everlasting life.
> **John 3:16**

This most famous verse tells us that God memorialized His desire for you by adding something to it. **He gave His Son at Calvary so that He could have you.** The cross of Jesus is a perpetual memorial of God's giving. He understands the principle of giving to receive.

Let this widow's action guide you in **focusing God's attention on your desire.** Simply begin to mix giving with your prayer, and you will be amazed at how quickly God will give His attention to the thing you want.

Our List Grows Longer

- Hannah mixed her giving and praying together, and she moved the hand of God to open her closed womb.

- The widow at Zarephath mixed her giving and praying together, and she moved the hand of God into her empty barrel.

- Jephthah mixed his giving and praying together, and he moved the hand of God against his enemy.

- Cornelius mixed his giving and praying together, and he moved the hand of God to bring Simon Peter to his house.

- The poor widow of Mark 12 mixed her giving and praying together, and she moved the hand of God to give her what she wanted.

- Many Christians of our day are also mixing their giving and praying together to move the hand of God. The following testimony is a good example.

Dear Brother John,

I am the pastor of a small but rapidly growing church. Because of the small size of our church and the recession which has hit harder in Atlantic Canada than anywhere else in our nation, resulting in my being laid off from a very lucrative secular management position, **we desperately needed a financial breakthrough.**

After reading *Moving the Hand of God,** my wife and I made a memorial prayer vow for another income stream. I got up from the sofa after we prayed and walked to the kitchen. **The telephone rang,** and the call was a job offer for my wife from a government agency that just had a position open up. **Not only did God answer our memorial prayer in less than five minutes,** but also the return was three times more than the amount of the vow.

In addition, within two weeks, **one of our outstanding debts was miraculously cancelled.** Brother John, we thank God for you and continue to stand with you, believing and confessing God's promises for success.

R.P.
Halifax, Nova Scotia, Canada

---

*   *Breakthrough for Unanswered Prayer* is a new, revised edition of the book, *Moving the Hand of God,* first published in 1990.

7

It Works for Us

... they overcame him by ... the word of
their testimony. ...

Revelation 12:11

It is necessary for tangible proof to accompany
doctrine. The teacher must be able to manifest that which
he is teaching. In this chapter I will share a few of the many
memorial prayers my wife and I have made. These prayers
swiftly moved the hand of God to the point of our need.

Memorial Prayer Brings Bookings

Several years ago my wife and I gave up the pastorate
of a church in the midwest to start our traveling ministry.
We left behind the security of a regular salary and
everything it provided. When we departed, we had only
one speaking engagement booked.

Please realize that our move was not the adventure of
a couple of young kids. We had already reached mid-life.
I was forty-nine, and Pat was forty-eight. We knew that if
the new ministry failed, we would suffer for the rest of our
lives.

Two months before we left, we made a significant
memorial prayer. **That memorial is still functioning as I
write this chapter many years later.**

At the time of our departure, the equity in our lovely home represented the greater portion of our assets. We had put $45,000 down on the house. No one will argue that it would have made good business sense to sell the house and carefully guard the equity from the sale.

Instead of holding on to our equity, we decided to use it as the financial portion of a memorial prayer. We knew that our greatest need would not be $45,000 in the bank. **Our greatest need would be speaking engagements in good churches every week.** If we kept the $45,000, how far could it go? Why, even if we were careful, it would last only a short time. However, plenty of good speaking engagements would provide the income for many years to come.

We were facing the same decision you face every time the offering plate passes your way. Should you trust the money and what it can do for you, or should you trust your God and what He is able to do? **Thank God that we decided not to trust the money!**

We Trusted God

Yes, we gave the $45,000 equity in our home to the church we were leaving. We then boldly mixed it with our request for adequate bookings. We prayed, **"God, we must have quality bookings.** There must be speaking engagements every Sunday and Wednesday and as many days in between as possible." Well, only a few days passed before God began to move in a way above and beyond anything we had even imagined.

After resigning, we went immediately to my one and only speaking engagement. It was the annual convention of a large ministry. I spoke three times in that meeting and received a modest honorarium. On the last night of the meeting, **I went to the closing banquet without a single booking ahead of me.** I must admit, it was not the most confident evening of my life. Memories filled my head of the words several well-meaning people had spoken to me. Most of those who had known of my plan to leave the security of my pulpit had said **it would be a foolish move.** They told me I would not have enough quality bookings to make ends meet. Needless to say, their words were echoing in my head. Besides that, the devil was telling me I would soon see **I had wasted my $45,000, and memorial prayers did not really work.**

A Voice of Encouragement

The only positive note I heard that night was from my dear wife, Pat. She reminded me of the many times our God had proved faithful in answering our memorial prayers. She said our prayer had been memorialized, and **at that very moment, it was lingering in the presence of God, speaking to Him of our desire.**

At the close of that evening's activities, as we walked from the banquet hall, the pastor of a church in the area approached me. Almost apologetically he told me his church was a small one. He knew I would probably not come, but he had felt a strong leading from the Lord to ask me to minister to his congregation. He asked if I would consider coming to his church sometime in the future. When I said I would be glad to, he asked me when I thought that might be. Since the next day was Sunday, I asked, **"How about in the morning?"**

At first he did not believe I was serious, but I quickly assured him I was. **With that appointment, I had a place to speak on my first Sunday away from the pastorate.**

Later that night the evangelist whose convention I was attending called my room and invited me to go to South Africa for twenty-one days. We would leave the following Friday. He also included my wife and son in the invitation. As I looked at my calendar, I was pleasantly surprised to see that **God had booked me solid for the entire month.**

God was still at work on our memorial. When I reached South Africa, an influential preacher there invited me to stay and preach an extra week. As we left, he invited me back and promised he would have places for me to preach every day for a month.

To make a long story short, in the first six months of our new ministry, **we never missed a Sunday or Wednesday night** of speaking, and we also spoke most of the nights in between. Not only that, but our bookings have never dropped below six months in advance since that day.

As I now write, **our calendar is solidly booked for over one year in advance.** When I say solidly booked, I mean almost every day of every month. At the time of this writing, I am home only an average of five days per month. It has truly happened to us as it happened to Cornelius. God is holding our gift and prayer in continual remembrance. I am pleased to report that the memorial of $45,000 we made those many years ago is still working. **It's working even better than we could have asked or thought.**

Paying Off an Office Building

In the early years of our traveling ministry, we purchased a new office building. We had quickly outgrown the space we were using in our house. Then in less than six months, we outgrew a rented facility.

The new building we purchased was beautiful, spacious, and conveniently located. When we moved in, it was much larger than we needed. In order to purchase the building, we had to take out a $225,000 loan. I had planned to rent out the part of the building we were not using to effect an early payoff of the note.*

Just before we moved in, a precious minister friend of ours told us she was moving her ministry to the Fort Worth area. She related that she was under tremendous financial pressure at the time. She said her office furniture was already in transit to our city and asked if we knew of any economical office space available.

Pat and I immediately saw her need as a tremendous opportunity for us. We quickly decided to make available to her the office space she needed. We told her we would do it without any rental cost to her.

---

* For information on how to pay off your mortgage rapidly, see *Rapid Debt-Reduction Strategies,* available from HIS Publishing Co., Ft. Worth, TX 76117-9001.

Rent Money or Early Payoff

Now you may ask, "How could you call that an opportunity? What you needed was rent money to help make the new mortgage payment."

Child of God, open your spiritual ears! The rent from the office space would only help make the monthly payments. **Our real desire was to pay off the entire mortgage as rapidly as possible.** We needed to build a memorial prayer for an early payoff of the $225,000 loan. I hope you can see that the need for a memorial prayer was much more important to our future than a few hundred dollars a month for the mortgage payment.

Now, don't misunderstand. The rent money would have alleviated pressure from our budget. It would have given us a much-needed cash flow, for we still had to purchase furniture and equipment to utilize the new building effectively.

Thank God, we had the wisdom to move her into the office rent-free! **It is my privilege to report that we paid off the balance on our mortgage in less than eighteen months.** Yes, you read correctly. It was miraculously paid in full. Even if we had charged our friend a thousand dollars per month in rent, it would have helped us make only a part of our monthly mortgage payment. However, by making the office space into the giving portion of a memorial prayer, **we moved the hand of God to a miracle payoff of the entire balance of the mortgage.**

A Better Retirement Plan

Pat and I recently made another memorial prayer. It had to do with our retirement.

When a responsible person reaches his fifties, he becomes fully aware of the approaching time when he will no longer be able to work. Pat and I have no plans or any desire for retirement, but we do know a time is coming when we will at least want to slow down. When that happens our earning potential will decrease.

After we checked into various retirement plans, we found a one-payment life insurance policy. With that form of insurance, you pay a single payment to a reputable insurance company, and it insures your life until you are sixty-five years old. At that time it pays you a large sum of money.

We thought this plan would give us enough income at age sixty-five for us to continue to minister without having to work quite so hard as we do now. When we saw the amount it would cost, we were astounded! **The premium would consist of a one-time payment of $104,000 cash.** Wow! That's a lot of money! However, the amount was not the most important thing we had to consider. The most pressing thing is that retirement age is fast approaching.

With some serious pencil work, we realized that if we liquidated some of our assets, we could obtain the needed premium. However, when we looked closely at the dollars the policy would make available to us at age sixty-five, especially after figuring in for several years of inflation, we realized it would not do so much for us as we had thought.

Suddenly it came to us! **We would invest the $104,000 in a memorial offering for our retirement.** We just knew God would bring us something better than the insurance company would. With that idea in mind, we gave the $104,000 into a good-ground ministry that understands memorial prayer. It was the largest single gift we had ever given to any one ministry.

It is with real joy that I write the next few words, for God has now revealed a financial plan of action that is quickly out-earning the $104,000 insurance plan. **Thank God for the wisdom He gave us to put memorial prayer to work for our retirement instead of an insurance company.**

Please don't misunderstand. God is not against insurance. He is not against retirement plans. Pat and I simply believed God would lead us to something better than the plan the world system had suggested.

Don't Be Scared Off

Before I scare someone away with the $45,000 and the $104,000 memorials, let me assure you that we have made memorial prayers with much smaller amounts. Even though the dollar amount of many of these was much less, please realize that **at the time we gave them,** they represented just as much to us as the larger gifts did.

Let me emphasize that there is not a set dollar amount that will move the hand of God in memorial prayer. It is what the amount of your offering means to you that makes it move God's hand. The gifts Pat and I now give are no larger in God's sight than the gifts we gave when we had almost nothing. Remember, it is the world that judges your offering by the amount of money you give. **God always judges it by how much you have left after you have given.** That truth is evident from Jesus' statement about the widow who threw in her two mites.

> ... this poor widow hath cast more in, than
> all they which have cast into the treasury:
> For ... she of her want did cast in all that
> she had, even all her living.
>
> Mark 12:43,44

Memorials Reach Beyond Financial Needs

Several years ago my second daughter experienced a tragic divorce. It seemed as if her life would never get straightened out. She and her three daughters had to move into the house with us, and she became dependent on us for a portion of her daily living.

Not only did she have the regular needs that go with caring for three children, she also needed to complete her education. As she went to school, the pressure from her situation became more and more evident. Even with all we were doing to help, she and her children were suffering a terrible void. We tried to be all we could to her, but it just wasn't enough. **She needed a good helpmate, and her children desperately needed a loving father.**

One day as we ministered in Mexico, my wife said, "John, what our daughter needs is a good husband. He must love her and help her and also love our precious grandchildren as if they were his own. **Let's make a memorial prayer before God for the right man to come into her life,** a special man who will make the whole family happy."

I asked how much she thought we could give. After calculating the balance in our checkbook, **she said we had about three hundred dollars left in our account.** With this valuable three hundred dollars, we decided to make a memorial for our daughter's new husband.

As we kneeled at the bed in our little Mexican hotel room, we carefully worded our prayer. We were very specific. We rehearsed all the good qualities and characteristics we expected our new son-in-law to have. Then we took the money and said, "We establish this memorial before God, and we trust His Word that it will be continually before Him until He sends the right man to our precious Sherri."

Well, I have seldom seen God work faster. Before the month was over, a fine man came into our daughter's life. He was everything we had ever asked for and more. As I write this, my daughter is now happily married to him. **He is a good husband, father, and son-in-law.** Since they have been married, they have both come to work for our ministry. In a day when many second marriages are worse than the first, we can explain his appearance in our lives in only one way. **The hand of God brought Charlie to our daughter, her children, and our ministry.**

An Old Feud Was Settled

Here is another illustration of a memorial prayer my wife and I built. Because of the delicacy of the subject, I will not be able to give many details, but I am sure this story will bless you.

For several years, my wife had a less-than-smooth relationship with a certain family member. I am not saying they fought all the time, but for one reason or another, there was always friction between them.

One day we found out this relative was coming to visit us for a long stay. At first my wife became tense, but then she quickly said, "I am going to move the hand of God into this situation. **We are going to be the best of friends."**

With that said, she made out a check for $250 and prayed, "Lord, I am making a memorial prayer before you this day. This relative and I are going to become friends — good friends! We will learn to flow together. **The devil will not cause friction between us any longer!"**

Thank God! There has never again been a cross word spoken between them! That visit was the best ever, and now they can hardly wait to speak and visit with each other.

Let me say that there is not enough space in this book to share every memorial prayer we have made. I have shared only a few. Memorial prayer has worked for us many times. It is working for us at this very moment and will continue working for us until Jesus returns.

I do hope these examples have been confirmation to you. My wife and I can, without hesitation, recommend this wonderful method of prayer to everyone. **Our hope is that memorial prayer will produce results for you as it has for us.**

> **. . . that we may be able to comfort them which are in any trouble, by the comfort wherewith we ourselves are comforted of God.**
> **2 Corinthians 1:4**

Before going to the next chapter, take a moment to read the following testimony.

Dear Brother John,

A friend suggested that I read any book I could find by John Avanzini. I went to our local bookstore and ordered *Moving the Hand of God.**

I had never heard of memorial prayer, but we had a friend in a difficult situation in which the hand of God was the only answer.

As a result, my wife and I gave a memorial offering for our friend who had cancer and was not given much hope to live. Her husband and several of us met with one of your staff members and prayed for her healing. You and your wife prayed for her, sent flowers, and the staff member called and prayed with her. Several leaders in our Amway business prayed for her healing as well.

Today this woman is completely healed and enjoying her five children again (ages one to eight). Thank God and thank you, Brother John. Memorial prayer works!

D.D.
Champaign, IL

---

*   *Breakthrough for Unanswered Prayer* is a new, revised edition of the book, *Moving the Hand of God,* first published in 1990.

8

It Will Work for You

For as many as are the promises of God,
THEY ALL FIND THEIR YES [ANSWER] IN
HIM....

2 Corinthians 1:20, Amplified

Yes, memorial prayer is going to work for you, not because I say it, but **because the Word of God says it.** Before you finish this chapter, you will be just as convinced of this truth as I am.

On the next few pages, you will find five things about God that never change. They are His special attitudes that guarantee you the right to use memorial prayer in your life. Your knowledge of these five things will quickly cast down any thought or opposition that rises up to deny you this privilege.

God Doesn't Play Favorites

I know memorial prayer will work for you **because the God you serve is not a respecter of persons.** He loves you just as much as He loves any other Christian. His Word declares His fairness in this matter.

And Peter opened his mouth and said: Most certainly and thoroughly I now perceive and understand THAT GOD SHOWS NO

PARTIALITY AND IS NO RESPECTER OF PERSONS.

Acts 10:34, Amplified

This verse declares something important to you. It tells you that if He has granted the privilege of using memorial prayer to any other person, God must also grant that privilege to you.

God Doesn't Hold Back the Good Things

Memorial prayer is a good thing. Scripture plainly testifies to this fact. To name just a few examples, Hannah, Jephthah, the widow at Zarephath, and Cornelius all received good things through memorial prayer. Testimonies from Christians around the world agree.

God's Word is clear. **He won't hold back any good thing from His obedient children.**

. . . NO GOOD THING WILL HE WITHHOLD from them that walk uprightly.

Psalm 84:11

If you are walking uprightly before your God, you have the right to the good things. He will not withhold them from you. Memorial prayer is a good thing, and God says it's yours.

God Wants You to Be Triumphant and Victorious

Memorial prayer brings triumph and victory to those who use it. From cover to cover, the Bible tells the stories of those who mixed their praying and giving to achieve dominion over the devil and their circumstances. These testimonies go even beyond the pages of the Bible. This book records several testimonies of people who triumphed victoriously over their enemies.

God openly declares that His best for you is to **triumph over your enemies and walk in total victory.**

> ... thanks be unto God, WHICH ALWAYS CAUSETH US TO TRIUMPH IN CHRIST. ...
> 2 Corinthians 2:14

> ... thanks be to God, which giveth us the victory through our Lord Jesus Christ.
> 1 Corinthians 15:57

Memorial prayer is triumphant prayer. It brings victory when nothing else will. **If God allowed it to work for others, surely He will allow it to work for you.**

God Has Something Better for You

There is yet another reason memorial prayer will work for you. God has promised He has better things for you than the Old Testament saints had. The writer dedicated the entire Book of Hebrews to this truth. In it God promises you a better hope, better testament, better covenant, better promises, and even a better sacrifice. Let me say it this way. Whatever good thing He did for Hannah, the widow at Zarephath, or Jephthah in the Old Testament, the writer of Hebrews says God will do even better for you today.

> God . . . PROVIDED SOME BETTER THING FOR US. ...
> Hebrews 11:40

If it worked for Old Testament saints, memorial prayer will work even better for you today.

God Never Changes

A final proof that memorial prayer will work for you is that our great God never changes. **If He did a thing before, He'll do it again!**

> For I am the Lord, I CHANGE NOT. . . .
> **Malachi 3:6**

> Jesus Christ the same yesterday, and to day, and for ever.
> **Hebrews 13:8**

God is the same today as He has always been. What He has done for others, He will surely do for you.

Let these five Bible guarantees settle the matter once and for all. Memorial prayer is scriptural, it's powerful, and it's yours. **Yes, memorial prayer will work for you!**

9

The Scope of Memorial Prayer

I am sure there must be a special need in your life, one you desire God to answer speedily. In this chapter you will find a few needs that seem to be common among Christians. In no way is this list intended to represent all the needs that exist. It simply mentions a few.

It Will Work With Your Children

It may be that your memorial prayer **will be for a wayward child.** The devil enjoys a double benefit when our children choose to operate outside the will of God. Not only does he ruin their lives, but he also causes them to break our hearts.

Everywhere I go, I find parents who need to move God's hand into the lives of their children. Maybe your need is for the restoration or salvation of your children. The mixing together of your praying and giving can change that situation. **It has moved the hand of God to bring two of our own children back from the edge of destruction, and even as I write, every one of our five children is in Christ and in full time ministry.**

If you have wayward children, **do not let go of them.** Build a memorial prayer before your God, one that will move His hand to snatch them out of the clutches of the devil. Begin to speak boldly to your God about them. Tell

Him of the need for their deliverance. **Then add giving to that prayer.** As you mingle your generous offering with your prayer of intercession, let God's Word be a comfort to you, for it tells you that memorial prayers are kept perpetually before God. Remember what the story of Cornelius told us. Prayers mingled with giving take up a perpetual position before God.

> ... thy prayer is heard, and thine alms are
> had in remembrance in the sight of God.
> **Acts 10:31**

A Better Standard of Living

Maybe your problem is that you just don't have enough money! Every month you believe your quality of life will be a bit better. **Then, month after month you fail to see any significant change.** The car you drive gets older. You have to wear the same clothing another month without replacement. The chance of your children receiving a proper education grows weaker with each passing year. You know your job has no hope of advancement. To put it in just a sentence, **you need your needs met in a much better way.**

Don't despair. You can do something about this situation. Someone wants your living standard improved as much as you do. It is your God. He wants you properly funded and abundantly supplied.

> ... his divine power hath given unto us ALL
> **THINGS THAT PERTAIN UNTO LIFE AND
> GODLINESS.** ...
> **2 Peter 1:3**

This day you can form a memorial prayer that will bring you into the quality lifestyle you desire. God wants it full of the good things you need and want. Remember, there is no scriptural reason for you to go through life without a good standard of living. The Bible says **the good life is your God-given portion.**

> **Behold . . . it is good and comely for one to eat and to drink, and to enjoy the good of all his labor that he taketh under the sun all the days of his life, which God giveth him: FOR IT IS HIS PORTION.**
> **Ecclesiastes 5:18**

Start right now to speak your desire for a better job, better house, better car, and especially a better future for you and your family. The powerful truth about memorial prayer can quickly place your petition before God, and just that quickly bring the financial deliverance you so desperately need.

It Will Bring the Right Mate

In the day in which we live, there are millions of broken homes. Single mothers are raising almost half the children in the United States. These mothers come from all walks of life. Many of them are Christian women. My heart goes out to these special saints who need good Christian mates.

My dear, single friend, it's time for you to make a memorial prayer **for your perfect mate.** I am convinced God will bring forth the man who is just right for you. Begin to speak to Him about your desire, for **He understands the memorial prayers of single women.** Remember how quickly He moved His hand into the barrel of meal for the widow at Zarephath. It happened as soon as she added giving to her praying. He also immediately turned His ear to the widow with the two mites when she gave. Surely He will hear you when you approach Him with your own memorial prayer.

Let me add that this same type of prayer will also bring **quick results for single men** who desire God's choice in a mate.

It Will Work at the Brink of Disaster

Even as you read these words, you may be **at the very brink of disaster.** Friend, let me tell you. God's hand can move when time is short. A deadline may be facing you. You may encounter a mountain in your path and want it moved immediately. It may already be **the eleventh hour and your high-noon encounter with the devourer but a moment away.**

Oh! Please remember Jephthah, for the same kind of problem faced him. The enemy was about to slaughter his entire army. The arm of flesh had failed him. His friends had walked out on him. In a decisive, last-minute attempt to move the hand of God, he supercharged his prayer with a sincere promise. It was a desperate moment. There wasn't even **time to make his offering.** All he had time for was to **make a pledge.**

It may be you don't have time to give your offering. You will just have to **call out your vow to God quickly.** I have seen people do that many times, and God has moved again and again.

Be careful when you vow! I have also seen something dangerous take place. Some folks can make vows to God in the day of emergency. Then later on they do not pay them.

I will never forget the following illustration of this danger. A number of years ago, I stood at the hospital bedside of a young man who had been in a horrible automobile accident. The doctors gave no hope for his survival. He was literally breathing the last breaths of life. At this moment I heard the boy's father make a memorial prayer that immediately moved God's hand into the room. He cried, **"O God! Save my son's life, and I will serve you all the days of my life!"**

The boy's vital signs suddenly improved. The doctors began to take hope, and miraculously, the boy lived. However, the father never kept his vow.

That man should have known better, for several years earlier he had faced a terrible divorce. He came to me and vowed to give our church a large amusement park he owned if only God would save his marriage. He went so far as to bring the deed for the property and sign it over to the church. Almost immediately thereafter, his wife came home to patch things up. **Within a few days of her return, he asked me to give him back the deed.** He said he could not keep his promise. A short time later his wife moved out and finalized the divorce. That marriage failed because he did not keep the vow of his memorial prayer.

Today that man is in prison, serving a life sentence for murder. When he committed the crime, people of the community couldn't believe it. They wondered how a leading citizen could have murdered someone. However, I (his pastor) knew. **You see, he failed to pay his vow to God,** and in so doing, he drew to himself the name that God has given to those who vow and do not pay.

> **When thou vowest a vow unto God, DEFER
> NOT TO PAY IT; for he hath no pleasure in
> fools: pay that which thou hast vowed.**
> **Ecclesiastes 5:4**

He became a fool, and now he lives where fools live.

I always caution those who make vows to keep them. However, don't let this warning keep you from making a memorial prayer with a vow. Just as He heard Hannah and accepted her vow, God will accept yours. Just be sure you keep the vow you make.

It's Time to Act

Child of God, **I know you are now convinced** that memorial prayer works and that it will work for you. You must now step out in faith and form your own memorial prayer. **The next few chapters will lead you step by step in making your memorial prayer, and in making it an effective one.**

10

Forming the Prayer of
Your Memorial

THOU SHALT MAKE THY PRAYER unto
him, and he shall hear thee, and thou shalt pay
thy vows.
.... and it shall be established unto thee....
Job 22:27,28

John the Baptist had to teach his disciples how to pray.
In the same way, Jesus had to teach His disciples.

... Lord, teach us to pray, as John also
taught his disciples.
Luke 11:1

Jesus also had to instruct His disciples in forming
different kinds of prayer such as the kind needed to cast
out certain evil spirits.

...Why could not we cast him out?
And he said unto them, This kind can come
forth by nothing, BUT BY PRAYER AND
FASTING.
Mark 9:28,29

It is the same with memorial prayer. You must learn
how to construct it properly. I have written this chapter for
that purpose.

71

Constructing Your Memorial Prayer

Let's look again at our opening verse for this chapter.

> THOU SHALT MAKE THY PRAYER unto him, and he shall hear thee, and THOU SHALT PAY THY VOWS.
> THOU SHALT ALSO DECREE A THING, and it shall be established unto thee. . . .
> **Job 22:27,28**

The gift part of the memorial prayer in these verses is a vow (a sincere promise). The petition part of this prayer is unspoken, or at least undisclosed, for the writer says only "thou shalt decree a thing. . . ."

Notice that the words *make thy prayer* aren't speaking of the wording of your prayer, but **of the construction of your prayer.** They speak of mixing together the gift and the decree.

Let's focus on the word *decree.* Scripture rarely uses this word. It appears in only a few places. In one place decree is interpreted **"to snatch a thing"** (Isaiah 9:20). It is easy to see a relationship between this interpretation and some of the Bible characters we have studied in this book, for it speaks of taking possession of something with violent action.

> . . . the kingdom of heaven suffereth violence, and THE VIOLENT TAKE IT BY FORCE.
> **Matthew 11:12**

Surely Hannah became violent as she began to speak to God about being forgotten. The widow at Zarephath became violent when she gave her last meal to the man of God. Without a doubt, the widow with the two mites showed violent action as she threw all her money into the offering.

If you construct your memorial prayer in this way, by mixing together your gift and your decree, God assures you of the answer. The Bible says, "**. . . it shall be established unto thee. . . .**"

What a wonderful word the Holy Spirit chose when He used the word *established.* It's an ancient Hebrew word that denotes several strong actions. It means **"the thing you demanded will be accomplished."** It can also mean **"the thing that is bad will be made good."** It further means **"the thing that needed to be done will be performed."** Finally, it means **"those things that oppose you will not oppose you any longer.** God will rise up against them."

The Petition

Let's now focus on forming the decree of your memorial prayer. What is it that you so desperately want or need? It may be something you have prayed about many times. If you recall, it was this type of situation that Hannah and the widow at Zarephath struggled with for such a long time. Both of these dear saints felt as if their heaven had turned to brass, bouncing their prayers back to them as quickly as they had called them out.

You may need an immediate answer like Jephthah. There may not be a single moment to waste.

There is also the possibility that your petition is unspoken like that of the widow who cast her two mites into the treasury. Sometimes our desires are of such a personal nature that we cannot share them with just anyone. **They are for the Savior's ears alone, for no one else would understand.**

Always Pray God's Will

It is important to understand that God will not answer a prayer just because you have attached money to it. **You cannot buy or bribe God.** It is clear from Scripture that He does not answer prayers contrary to His will.

> And this is the confidence that we have in him, that, IF WE ASK ANY THING ACCORDING TO HIS WILL, he heareth us.
> 1 John 5:14

Pray the Word

Praying according to God's will is not so hard as it seems. If you are praying for a lost person, pray **first and foremost for that person's salvation,** because God's Word says He doesn't want anyone to perish.

> The Lord is ... NOT WILLING THAT ANY SHOULD PERISH, but that all should come to repentance.
> 2 Peter 3:9

If you are praying for financial deliverance, **boldly ask for the money you need.** Ask with confidence, knowing it is God's desire for you to prosper.

> Beloved, I wish above all things THAT THOU MAYEST PROSPER and be in health, even as thy soul prospereth.
> 3 John 2

If your prayer is about a brother or sister in Christ, **pray only those things that will uplift** and bring him or her into the center of God's will.

> So let us then definitely aim for and eagerly pursue what makes for harmony and for MUTUAL UPBUILDING (EDIFICATION AND DEVELOPMENT) OF ONE ANOTHER.
> Romans 14:19, Amplified

Clearly and Boldly

As you now form the petition (the request part) of your memorial prayer, be sure to **state clearly the thing you desire.** Give as much thought as possible to what the Bible says about it. It is always good to have a Bible verse or references that agree with or parallel the thing for which you are asking.

There must also be boldness in your prayer. **You must not be sheepish.** You must speak with authority when you make your petition known.

> Seeing then that we have a great high priest . . . Jesus the Son of God . . . .
> Let us therefore COME BOLDLY UNTO THE THRONE OF GRACE. . . .
> Hebrews 4:14,16

Be sure to write out your petition so that you won't miss anything. Because of the extreme closeness that will exist **between your prayer and your offering,** go immediately to the next chapter, where I will show you **step by step** how to decide on the amount of money that is to become part of your memorial prayer.

11

Determining the Money of Your Memorial

> . . . this . . . shall be spoken of for a
> memorial of her.
> **Mark 14:9**

The exactness of God's Word is astounding. It never leaves you guessing about important things. The fourteenth chapter of Mark gives detailed information about the money for a memorial. The instructions are **clear, concise,** and **easy to follow.**

The Gift Must Be Valuable to You

In Mark 14 we find a woman who performs an act that becomes a memorial. She anoints Jesus with an extremely valuable, perfumed oil.

> . . . there came a woman having an alabaster
> box of ointment of spikenard very precious; and
> she brake the box, and poured it on his head.
> **Mark 14:3**

It is difficult to place a value in today's currency on the ointment. However, Mark tells us it was worth **over three hundred pence.**

> **For it might have been sold for more than**
> **THREE HUNDRED PENCE....**
> **Mark 14:5**

Three hundred pence was about two-thirds of the annual wages for an average laborer. Probably the most accurate way to describe the worth of the ointment is to say **it was very valuable.**

Upon reading the whole discourse, you will find there was disapproval among those who stood by when she poured this most expensive oil upon our Lord. Some called it a waste. However, Jesus Himself established the true value of her gift. He said **she had done a good thing.**

> **And Jesus said, Let her alone; why trouble**
> **ye her? SHE HATH WROUGHT A GOOD**
> **WORK ON ME.**
> **Mark 14:6**

You Cannot Do Everything

Those who found fault with the way she used the oil were quick to point out that her act was a selfish one. Why, the poor needed it more than Jesus did.

You must learn something here. One of the devil's favorite tricks for stopping the abundance of God from coming to you is simply to **redirect** your giving. If he cannot stop you from giving, he will try to have you give **differently from how God is directing you.**

For as long as I can remember, there have always been a hundred good places for the money every time my wife and I were ready to give. Keep this next thought in mind. **Before you can do anything, you will have to realize you cannot do everything.** Each time you make a memorial prayer, there will be many other important things you need to do. Don't you know that the little widow with two mites (Mark 12) had a long list of things she could have done with her money? However, she decided this time she would spend it in making a memorial prayer. **This time it would be for the thing she desired.**

The Most Not the Least

Jesus made a statement about the gift of the woman with the box of ointment that clearly tells us how much money a person making a memorial should give. He said **she did as much as she could.**

> **She hath done what she could: she is come aforehand to anoint my body to the burying.**
> **Mark 14:8**

This simple statement gives us the formula for establishing the money of every memorial prayer that would ever follow hers. It fairly settles the amount the rich, as well as the poor, should give. Every person must simply give all he can.

You will never memorialize your prayer **by giving the least you can,** or even by giving **more than the average person.** The money of your memorial must be of such importance in your eyes **that it projects to our Lord the urgency of your request,** as well as the **sincerity of your heart.**

God Is Moved As You Are Moved

Few Christians give any thought to how God places a value on their offerings. They assume a hundred thousand dollars is a large amount to God, and a dollar is a small amount to Him. They never consider that God owns everything and wants for no material possession whatsoever. Because of His unlimited wealth, He has chosen to establish the size of an offering, not by the amount the person gives, but **by how much he has left after he has given.** A hundred thousand dollars from a person who has three billion dollars is a much smaller gift in God's eyes than one dollar from a person **who has only one dollar.**

> . . . this poor widow hath cast more in . . . .
> **For all they did cast in of their abundance**
> **[excess funds]; but she . . . CAST IN ALL THAT**
> **SHE HAD. . . .**
> Mark 12:43,44

Here is a good rule to follow when establishing how much to give. **If the gift you give is insignificant to you, it will be insignificant to God.** Scripture tells us that whatever moves us will move God.

> **For we have not an high priest which cannot**
> **be touched with the feeling of our infirmities. . . .**
> Hebrews 4:15

He feels what you feel. He draws His opinion about your offering from **the way you feel about it.** The more you think about this verse, the more convinced you will become that He judges your actions primarily by the way you feel about them. If the amount you give **does not impress you, it will not impress Him.** If your gift represents **little value to you, it will be of little value to Him.**

Establishing an Eternal Memorial

Not until verse nine do we understand how much value our Lord places upon this woman's alabaster box of ointment.

> **Verily I say unto you, Wheresoever this gospel shall be preached throughout the whole world, this also that she hath done shall be spoken of for a memorial of her.**
> **Mark 14:9**

Make no mistake about it, God Jehovah could create an entire ocean of oil of spikenard. He could gather all the oil of spikenard in the world with only a word. When you consider this fact, it is clear that **the value the woman placed on the oil established its worth to God.** Scripture doesn't say the oil of spikenard was very precious to Jesus, but to the woman. **Because it was precious to her, it immediately became precious enough to Him to memorialize her act of giving forever.**

> **. . . Wheresoever this gospel shall be preached throughout the whole world, this also that she hath done shall be spoken of for a memorial of her.**
> **Mark 14:9**

Notice that this woman did not build a church. She did not lead a large crusade. She did not write one of the books of the Bible. Nevertheless, every Christian who ever lived has known her. Try to grasp how valuable her gift was for it to have generated a perpetual memorial of her act of worship to our Lord. **This kind of giving will memorialize your prayer.** As our Lord said, the amount must be significant to you. **It must be all you can do.**

81

She hath done WHAT SHE COULD. . . .
Mark 14:8

Determining Your Offering

You must now evaluate just how important the request of your memorial prayer is to you. This evaluation must guide you in determining how much you will give as the offering. Please remember that Jesus said the woman did all she could. He didn't say she did the least she could. As you prayerfully consider the amount of your gift, at some point **you will feel peace begin to come over you.** God's Word says His peace will come upon you and work **as an umpire** to tell you when your gift is proper.

> . . . let the peace (soul harmony which comes) from Christ rule (ACT AS UMPIRE CONTINUALLY) in your hearts [deciding and settling with finality all questions that arise in your minds] . . . .
> Colossians 3:15, Amplified

Three Methods of Giving

With Scripture as a guide, you can use three types of offerings when making a memorial prayer. They are the vow, the immediate offering, and the segmented offering.

The Vow

A vow is nothing more than a solemn promise. Two of those who offered memorial prayers in Scripture used vows. They were Hannah and Jephthah. As you remember, Hannah gave a vow as her offering because the gift she offered was a son she had not yet conceived. Jephthah vowed because he was far from his home and possessions. The enemy was coming in like a flood. There wasn't time to go home and get his offering. Because of the distance, he simply vowed to give when he returned.

Either one of these reasons is acceptable in making your offering with a vow. If for some reason you don't have the amount you want to give, you can make a vow or as some call it, **"a faith promise."** Your earnest intention will be to pay it as soon as you have it. Let me caution you again about this kind of giving. Please remember that while vows are fully acceptable to Him, God does give a warning to those who choose to use them. He says if you do not pay your vow, **He will look upon you as a fool.**

> **When thou vowest a vow unto God, defer not to pay it; FOR HE HATH NO PLEASURE IN FOOLS: pay that which thou hast vowed.**
> **Ecclesiastes 5:4**

Vowing is a legitimate way to give to God if you are without funds, or if you are far away from your funds. You may also give with a promise if you have to **transfer funds, sell stock,** or **sell property.** Just remember, you must pay a vow made to God as quickly as possible.

The Immediate Offering

The widow with two mites gave an immediate offering. She took what she had and gave it to the Lord. This type of offering is simple to give. It **immediately** expresses the sincerity of your heart.

If you are giving your gift as an immediate offering, **be careful that it fully conveys your innermost feelings** about your prayer request. Sometimes it is possible to give a convenient amount instead of one which conveys the intensity of your desire. When you give an immediate offering, be sure it is a significant amount to you, for if it is not, it will not be significant to our Lord.

The Segmented Offering

The segmented offering **is made in payments.** Cornelius and the widow at Zarephath used this type of giving to turn their prayers into memorials.

At first glance it may not seem that the widow at Zarephath gave in this way. However, upon close examination you will find that she gave to Elijah **every day.** Yes, you are reading correctly. The Word of God says her giving was done in segments. She gave continually until the famine ended.

> **And she went and did according to the saying of Elijah: and she, AND HE [ELIJAH], and her house, did eat many days.**
> **1 Kings 17:15**

The segmented giving of Cornelius is more obvious, for Scripture tells us he gave often.

> **A devout man . . . which gave much alms. . . .**
> **Acts 10:2**

These two examples of segmented giving show clearly that it is a legitimate form of giving in making a memorial prayer.

It may be that segmented giving is the only way you will be able to give the amount your heart is telling you to give. **It may be that you want to give a thousand dollars,** but it seems impossible for you to give such an amount in a lump sum. **Don't despair.** My wife and I had that same feeling the first time we wanted to give a thousand dollars.

We did exactly as the widow at Zarephath did. **We simply segmented the thousand dollars into fifty payments of twenty dollars per week.** Yes, it took a year for us to pay it, but we did it.

God's Word in no way discourages making payments to Him. The Bible actually teaches it. Notice that **the Philippian church chose to send payments to Paul.**

> **For even in Thessalonica ye sent ONCE AND AGAIN unto my necessity.**
> **Philippians 4:16**

If you will not be able to give the amount you feel impressed to give in a lump sum, go ahead and make the gift in payments.

You May Face Opposition

Many times well-meaning folks will rise up against you. Remember, they were against the woman with the alabaster box of ointment. I am sure many also rebuked the widow when she gave her last two mites. No doubt they told her she was foolish not to use the money to supply her own pressing needs. However, **there are times when your heart cries out for more than food and lodging.** Sometimes you must give whatever money you have to God. The Scripture clearly says, **"Man shall not live by bread alone"** (Matthew 4:4). When the widow gave it all to God, her desire simply outweighed her needs.

> **. . . she of her want did cast in ALL THAT SHE HAD. . . .**
> **Mark 12:44**

Be Settled

In determining the financial portion of your memorial, your heart must be firmly settled as to the amount you are to give. **Please do not lightly brush over this decision,** for if you don't make up your mind about the amount, Satan will cause you to switch back and forth between amounts. Then you will **diminish your ability to receive from God.**

> . . . let not that man think that he shall receive any thing of the Lord.
> A DOUBLE-MINDED MAN IS UNSTABLE in all his ways.
> **James 1:7,8**

When you have the peace of God about the amount, do not waiver. Let your spirit be settled and unchangeable.

You Must Be Determined

Determination is the forceful state of mind that does not allow you to stop doing what you have decided until you have completed it. **Determination kept Jesus on the road to Calvary.** Holy-Spirit-given energy brought the Apostle Paul's life to a victorious conclusion.

> **I have fought a good fight, I have finished my course, I have kept the faith.**
> **2 Timothy 4:7**

You must now rise up in confident determination and give the amount God's peace has confirmed to you. **Do it now, and do it exactly as God has directed you** by the blessed approval of the Holy Spirit.

Dear Brother John,

I attended your Baltimore School of Biblical Economics where I heard your teaching on memorial prayer. After reading your book, **Moving the Hand of God,*** I **established a memorial prayer which God answered in one week.**

We were looking for a larger house since we now have six children at home. We found a house in an area of Ohio that was almost what we needed, however, we could never seem to satisfy the requirements of the bank to purchase it. **We have good credit because we paid off our debts using your getting out of debt teachings,** and we had always paid our bills on time. For some reason the bank was procrastinating on our loan. Finally we said, "Let's make a memorial prayer." **We made a vow of ten thousand dollars to your ministry** over the telephone.

Almost immediately the hand of God began to move. I **made the vow on July 1, 1992.** On July 2nd, my pastor in Alabama talked with me and said that the Lord had informed him that we would be moving from Ohio back to Alabama. Since I was in Alabama visiting my family, I began to look for the house we had specified in our memorial prayer. I talked to a realtor and he informed me that his office was in the southern part of Alabama and that he would contact a realtor in the area where we were looking. **This was July 2, 1992.** The realtor called that evening about 7:00 P.M. to get our requirements.

The realtor called the next night about 8:00 P.M. and said she had found a house which met our requirements. I saw the house on Monday, July 6th, and made an offer on it. I waited twenty minutes for the seller to sign her name. By the following Monday the bank had approved the loan for the house. We moved into the exact house we wanted, and

---

* *Breakthrough for Unanswered Prayer* is a new, revised edition of the book, *Moving the Hand of God,* first published in 1990.

it was fifty thousand dollars cheaper than the original one. We wanted a five bedroom, three-bath house, with five to ten acres. This house has eight acres. We immediately dedicated it to the service of the Lord.

We moved into our new house on **August 6, 1992,** and **sent John Avanzini Ministries a check for ten thousand dollars a week later.** We saw God begin to move when we made that vow. **Memorial prayer worked for us.**

D.S.
Talledga, AL

12

Properly Placing Your Memorial

> And other FELL ON GOOD GROUND, and
> sprang up, and bare fruit. . . .
> Luke 8:8

One day the entire Body of Christ will understand memorial prayer. Every minister and every member of every local church will understand it as well as they now understand the Lord's Prayer. When this time comes, it will be simple to decide where to place your memorial prayer, for every ministry will be in agreement.

You Must Have Agreement

Even as the adding of giving to your prayer increases its power, **the adding of agreement will increase its power even more.**

> . . . I tell you, if two of you on earth AGREE
> (HARMONIZE TOGETHER, MAKE A
> SYMPHONY TOGETHER) about whatever
> [anything and everything] they may ask, IT
> WILL COME TO PASS AND BE DONE FOR
> THEM by My Father in heaven.
> Matthew 18:19, Amplified

I hope you realize it would be impossible for someone to agree, harmonize, or make a symphony with you over your memorial prayer **if that person did not fully understand it.**

89

Agreement in All Ways

It is important that agreement with your memorial prayer goes **beyond simply understanding the request portion.** There must also be an **understanding of the method of prayer you are using.** Remember, God is only now restoring memorial prayer to the Church. While those who have become weary of living with unanswered prayer have widely accepted it, **many religious leaders do not yet understand memorial prayer.**

Chosen by God's Grace

I must say that prayer has never been the strongest point of my anointing. **That is, until now,** for God has called on me to re-establish the truth of memorial prayer into His end-time Church. The situation in which I find myself must be much like the one in which the Apostle Paul found himself. God called him into the ministry, and then allowed him to write a major part of the New Testament. By his own admission he was chief of sinners, until God, by His sovereign grace, made him chief of saints.

Surely I was one of the poorest at praying, but **for some unexplainable reason, by the sovereign grace of God,** He has chosen me to reintroduce memorial prayer into His Church.

I Want to Agree With You

Because of this most undeserved honor, **I now make myself and those who are nearest to me available to you.** I have dedicated almost every waking moment of my life to the heavenly vision I have received from God.* It is a three-fold mandate that takes me daily into every part of the world. God specifically commissioned me to teach biblical economics, to lead in the war on debt, **and to help wipe out unanswered prayer through memorial prayer.** My wife and I, as well as my children, **pray daily** for each memorial prayer request we receive into our ministry. Every one of us understands and agrees with the principle of memorial prayer. We each use this powerful method of prayer in our own lives to move God's hand. **We lift every memorial prayer request up before the Lord daily for at least thirty days.** Our church congregation (International Faith Center in Fort Worth, Texas) also lifts them up every Sunday and Thursday during that thirty-day period.

Where the Money Goes

Every cent given into our ministry is totally tax deductible and finances the worldwide outreach of His Image Ministries. We are strictly governed by a Board of Advisors.

It Is Now Time for You to Act

Clearly state the petition you are making to the Father. **Keep a copy for yourself and send one to me.** Carefully determine the amount of money and the way in which you will give it. If you will be using a vow, **make sure you sincerely intend to keep it.** If you will give an immediate offering, be sure the amount **is significant to you** and adequately conveys the importance of your

---

* For details of this God-given vision, see *Hundredfold,* available from HIS Publishing Co., Ft. Worth, TX 76117-9001.

request to God. If you will be giving a segmented offering, **send the first part with your request** and faithfully fulfill the remaining payments. Please don't make the mistake of stopping before you have given the promised amount. Some people stop giving because their answer comes before they fulfill their promised offering. Others stop because they see no immediate results.

With your prayer request clearly written and the amount of your offering firmly fixed in your mind, place the gift and the prayer together before God. **Now earnestly pray over them and send them to me.** Pray daily in agreement with my family and me as we will pray each day with you. Continue to do so until the answer comes.

Tell Us When It Happens

When God blesses you with answers to your memorial prayers, **let us know immediately.** Don't wait until you see me in an airport, at a camp meeting, or at your local church. Let us know immediately when you receive the victory. **We are eager to hear your testimony so that we can praise God and rejoice with you.** Remember, we have been waiting and praying for the answer with you.

Until I hear from you . . . .

John Avanzini
c/o Partner Love Center
P.O. Box 917001
Ft. Worth, TX 76117-9001

Books by John Avanzini

Always Abounding $6.95
Enter a new dimension of abundant living through a plan
from God's Word that cannot fail.

Faith Extenders $8.95
Discover how you can use the methods of Abraham and
other Bible characters to increase your faith.

God's Debt-Free Guarantee $5.95
Learn the five simple steps that will add new power to your
out-of-debt program.

30-60-Hundredfold $8.95
See clearly the scriptural laws of seed-time and harvest,
God's plan for your increase. (Also available in Spanish)

It's Not Working, Brother John! $9.95
Find out twenty-five ways to keep the windows of heaven
open over your life. (Also available in Spanish)

John Avanzini Answers Your Questions $6.95
Find the answers to the twenty most-often-asked questions
about biblical economics.

Powerful Principles of Increase $7.95
Find out how you can take the resources of this world to
establish God's Kingdom.

Stolen Property Returned $5.95
See how to identify the thief, take him to the heavenly
courtroom, and recover what he has stolen.

Things That Are Better Than Money $5.95
Discover the things Scripture reveals that are more
valuable than money.

The Wealth of the World $7.95
Find help to prepare for your part in the great end-time
harvest of souls and of wealth.

**What Jesus Taught About
Manifesting Abundance** $5.95
Study the principles of the superabundant harvest that
Jesus taught in Mark 4.

The Financial Freedom Series

War on Debt $7.95
Financial Freedom Series, Volume I—If you are caught in
a web of debt, your situation is not hopeless. You can
break the power of the spirit of debt.

Rapid Debt-Reduction Strategies $12.95
Financial Freedom Series, Volume II—Learn practical
ways to pay off all your debts—mortgage included—in
record time.

The Victory Book $14.95
Financial Freedom Series, Volume III—This workbook
takes you step by step through The Master Plan for paying
off every debt.

Have a Good Report $8.95
Financial Freedom Series, Volume IV—Find out what
your credit report says about you, and learn the steps that
will help you correct negative information.

**Complete both sides of this order form
and return it to HIS Publishing Co.
to receive a 10% discount
on your book order.**

Qty	Title	Cost	Total
	Always Abounding	6.95	
	Faith Extenders	8.95	
	God's Debt-Free Guarantee	5.95	
	30-60-Hundredfold	8.95	
	It's Not Working, Brother John!	9.95	
	John Avanzini Answers Questions	6.95	
	Powerful Principles of Increase	7.95	
	Stolen Property Returned	5.95	
	Things Better Than Money	5.95	
	The Wealth of the World	7.95	
	What Jesus Taught	5.95	
	War on Debt	7.95	
	Rapid Debt-Reduction Strategies	12.95	
	The Victory Book	14.95	
	Have a Good Report	8.95	
	Subtotal		
	Less 10% Discount		
	Shipping & Handling		**2.00**
	Total Enclosed		

(1038)

( ) Enclosed is my check or money order made
payable to **HIS Publishing Company**

Please charge my: ( ) Visa ( ) MasterCard

( ) Discover ( ) American Express

Account # ☐☐☐☐☐☐☐☐☐☐☐☐☐☐☐☐

Expiration Date _____ / _____ / _____

Signature_____

To assure prompt and accurate delivery of your order,
please take the time to print all information neatly.

Name_____

Address_____

City_____State_____Zip_____

Area Code & Phone (_____)_____

Send mail orders to:

HIS Publishing Company

P.O. Box 917001

Ft. Worth, TX 76117-9001

I WANT TO HELP YOU WIN YOUR WAR ON DEBT!

It has taken a year of hard work and now all of the material for the Debt Free Army is ready to be placed in your hands.

Enlist Today And The Following Materials Will Be Immediately Sent To You:

YOUR PERSONAL ONE-OF-A KIND BATTLE PLAN PORTFOLIO WHICH INCLUDES:

A large 12-place, library-style audio cassette binder. •Your Battle Plan Notebook with 12 full-color dividers designed to index over 250 pages of Debt-Free Strategies. •"The First Thirty Days To Victory" - a comprehensive "Master Plan" designed to help you become debt free. •The Debt Free Army Ammunition. (Your first monthly audio tape of insight, inspiration, and motivation.) This is a personal one-on-one tape you will receive from Brother John each month.

GOD WANTS YOU TO BE DEBT FREE!

Now... through the Debt Free Army you can put His plan for your Debt-Free life-style into action.

As a member of the Debt Free Army, I will be able to personally guide you, step by step month by month, from the slavery of debt into the glorious experience of debt-free living. No matter what financial condition you're in, this strategically prepared material can take you steadily and rapidly out of debt. It's worked for others-it will work for you.

–John Avanzini

CALL TOLL FREE
1-800-FREE ARMY

 To receive your FREE copy of HOW TO SAVE BIG MONEY ON YOUR UTILITY BILLS

Now you can have your own personal copy of this valuable 8-page, full-color supplement taken directly from the Debt Free Army's Battle Plan arsenal. Included in this money-saving piece are **40 ways** you can save from **$30 to $80 each month** on your utility bills -- And it will be sent to you absolutely FREE and postage paid when you **call 1- 800 - FREE ARMY**